Oh Sheet!

Valerie Crowe

Archway Publishing books may be ordered through booksellers or by contacting:

Archway Publishing
1663 Liberty Drive
Bloomington, IN 47403
www.archwaypublishing.com
1 (888) 242-5904

Because of the dynamic nature of the Internet, any web addresses or links contained in this book may have changed since publication and may no longer be valid. The views expressed in this work are solely those of the author and do not necessarily reflect the views of the publisher, and the publisher hereby disclaims any responsibility for them.

Any people depicted in stock imagery provided by Getty Images are models, and such images are being used for illustrative purposes only. Certain stock imagery © Getty Images.

ISBN: 978-1-4808-7355-1 (sc)
ISBN: 978-1-4808-7356-8 (e)

Library of Congress Control Number: 2018968548

Print information available on the last page.

Archway Publishing rev. date: 01/11/2019

Contents

Preface

This collection of short essays is really my personal opinion on the world I am currently living in, which daily provides me with a great deal of entertainment mixed with a liberal smattering of exasperation.

Hopefully I have managed to convey some of that amusement without offending my family and friends, who, by their very existence, feature in many of the anecdotes. At least I have not mentioned any of them by name, but they know who they are, and I will probably hear about it at some time in the future.

Between the failure of fitted sheet folding, to a recommendation on why we should eat more chocolate, I am indebted to my family for not having me restrained. However, it's early days yet.

I hope that many of the readers will identify with some of the situations described and will be able to say with intense feeling, "This is so true." In that case, this short book will have fulfilled all my expectations. Just remember that life is short, and whether we want to complain about it or enjoy it is our choice.

Personally, I hope you choose to enjoy both this book and life.

—Valerie Crowe

Oh Sheet!

I know that it cannot just be me! I am totally convinced that my recent "Houdini" exploits in trying to fold a fitted sheet qualify as one of the most common complaints experienced by anyone who has to do a weekly load of laundry that involves bed linens.

I have watched countless YouTube videos on the art of folding these seemingly innocent objects, but as soon as I'm confronted with the wretched things, the nightmare starts again. I've tried laying them out on the bed and stretching out the corners, but as soon as I think I have one side under control, the other side curls up into a ball, and it's back to square one.

I have had former friends stand in front of me with one of these fitted sheets to walk me through the folding cycle while I mirror their actions, but as soon as I lose eye contact, the game is over. Now just how hard can this be? I end up with a crumpled heap of linen that closely resembles the hauled-down sails of a yacht. I am resigned to the fact that a pristine, folded, and crease-less fitted bedsheet is just not meant to reside in my laundry closet. Any fitted sheets in my house drape nicely over the closet door, thank you very much, or if I am expecting company, I have mastered the art of rolling them into a tight cylindrical shape and wedging them into the closet, accompanied by an assortment of pillowcases and those articles of linen called pillow shams!

So does a pillow sham mean that no real pillows are allowed inside the frilly casing? How did they get their name? Are the other pillowcases called pillow "reals"? There has to be a rhyme or reason behind this nomenclature, but having exhausted my energy trying to fold a fitted sheet, I have resigned myself to sheer acceptance.

If one has the strength after a day of linen wrestling, one *may* be tempted to try to qualify for the advanced post-laundry procedure known as "Stuff the Sack." For those among us who are only familiar with the boring single-layer quilt, or even blanket, this is an art to be mastered. It entails manipulating a seemingly enormous padded cover—or duvet, if you want to be posh—and trying to force it into a huge sack adorned with the in design of the moment and with a relatively small accessibility opening. (It is reminiscent of a well-endowed lady trying to fit into a minuscule training bra.)

There are people who swear by their own method, guaranteeing success. These methods vary between turning the sack inside out, laying the padded quilt/duvet out on top, and with a few deft movements, turning the whole mixture right side out with just a flick of the wrist. Just who are they kidding? There is also the time-honored method of trying to fit the padded cover through the teeny tiny opening and then crawling in after it to make sure the top corners get well and truly stuffed. I have found it nigh on impossible to accomplish this without losing my way inside the sack, or getting the inside part so crumpled that the whole effect is ruined by a huge bunched-up section of duvet that cannot be smoothed out without removing the whole thing and starting again, assuming you have the inclination and the energy. If you are unlucky enough to have a cover with buttons and buttonholes, do some deep-breathing techniques before attempting closure, because as sure as sheets, you will have more holes than buttons unless you are very, very careful.

The deep, cavernous depths of a duvet or quilt cover are also places where lost socks go to die! Maybe other items of clothing too. I have often tried to fathom the cause of a small, unyielding bump, usually dead center inside the cover. Just say a few prayers over it because it is gone, never to see the light of day again. Make your mind up. You will never be able to extract said object unless you intend to crawl inside, live there, and learn to love the bump in the duvet.

My advice to you all is to go with a single bottom sheet, a top sheet, and a blanket. Your bedroom may not look haute mode, but you will be sane, you will have all your fingernails, and you will have much more time for other pursuits.

Vertically Challenged

Okay, I'm short. I've never complained about it—much—and life goes on. However, it has come to my notice of late that there is a plot afoot to discriminate (now there's a hot word) against those who are commonly referred to as knee high to a grasshopper.

Let me give you a few examples. Our local movie theater has now reached grandiose status inasmuch as all the seating has been changed from the standard uncomfortable fold-up/fold-down type of seats to a luxurious set of recliners. *Fantastic,* I thought. Then I climbed into one and disappeared from view. From my companion's hysteria, apparently all that could be seen of me was a pair of feet waving in the gentle breeze of the air conditioner. It was a classic case of "her feet never touched the ground." To add insult to injury, one needs a one-on-one tuition course to master the art of the recliner controls, which I obviously hadn't attended. The reason I had decided to watch a movie in the theater rather than at home where the chairs fit me is because *usually* it's relatively relaxing. No need to manipulate four or five remotes because that's all taken care of for you. However, I certainly wasn't expecting to need a winch to get me out of the brand-new recliner.

It's the same with cabinets. I recently remodeled my kitchen. Fancy new cabinets that go all the way up to the ceiling. What was

I thinking? Did I think to order built-in step stools? Of course not. I have to fight with my small grandchildren to steal their little plastic stools that they need to reach the bathroom sink, and then maybe—just maybe—I may be able to reach the second level of shelving in my new kitchen. The third and fourth levels require an actual stepladder. Stands to reason I have no idea what's up there. It's so embarrassing, but there's a learning curve.

I hesitate to refer to genetics, but somewhere, I have misplaced the tall genes that should have been stored in my DNA. There's not a person in my family, or in my add-on family (in-laws, etc.), who isn't taller than me. Even my grandchildren are beginning to look down on me, and they're only just out of kindergarten. Really?

How many times have I heard the phrase, "Good things come in small parcels"? Not enough, I can tell you. The sad thing is that when I started in high school, I was one of the taller students, but then my body saw no good reason to move on up in the world so that by the time I graduated, I was one of the smallest in my year. Now I ask you, is that fair?

I need a step stool to clean windows (that's no real loss), a step stool to trim the best blossoms on my weeping hibiscus, and a step stool to reach the books in my library. (Do not ask when I last dusted the top shelves.) Forget changing light bulbs or coaxing spiders out from upper corners. Again, no real loss there either. My entire house has step stools randomly distributed throughout, because one never knows when one might need to broaden one's paradigms and venture beyond one's normal reach.

To keep myself out of trouble and to keep my airways open, I like choral singing. I have been allowed to sing in several church choirs, but I must also hasten to add that I am a back-up singer. For the less motivated in this world, I like to classify singers as those with the melody and those who chug along singing the church equivalent of doo-wop. This is just among the females in the choir, you understand; the male singers can sort out their own problems. Anyway, all this is leading up to the fact that in our choir room, there are three heights of chair. One for the nonvertically challenged, one for normal-sized choristers, and a lower-height chair for the others. I know instantly when my usual chair has been moved because my feet dangle in the air. Try keeping a beat by tapping your toes when they are struggling for any kind of purchase. It's getting to the stage where we need to be fitted for our chairs. How pathetic is that?

I have to mention trucks. There are several truck owners in my family, of which I am not one. I have a normal car made for people who are shorter than the average hulk. If your truck owner likes you, he or she may have installed an additional side rail/step so you can climb in without attracting too much attention. Do make sure you have on clean underwear when attempting to make this ascent, and take plenty of tissues to stop the occasional nosebleed. It's short on oxygen up there. If this installation (the side rail, not the clean underwear) is not immediately visible—call a taxi.

Yawn!

*A*fter years of having to get up early for whatever reason—work and children come rapidly to mind—when every fiber of my being is screaming at me to stay asleep, I have tried to perfect the art of staying in bed at least until the sun is well up. Why is it, then, that every activity that attracts me during my well-earned retirement kicks off at the crack of dawn?

I don't know about you, but I am not at my sharpest when it's still dark outside. For instance, have you noticed that flights to wherever one wants to visit when one is paying for them out of one's own ever-dwindling bank account are most economical at zero-dark-hundred? I am always amazed that the pilot can manage to keep both eyes open at this unearthly time of day. That should be called time of night anyway. Dark equates to sleep time in my book.

Such flights are often staffed by flight attendants who insist on inflicting a false *bonhomie* on the sleepy passengers while the attendants' immaculate makeup and usually unintelligible nasal-toned voice instills in me a sadistic urge to tell them that they have a piece of broccoli wedged in their front choppers. Kudos to a recent passenger who arrived for her very, very early flight dressed in a full bunny pajama suit complete with wee tail firmly attached to her rear. Bunny feet, hoodie, bunny ears, and all! (No whiskers, though … I was disappointed.) She just retreated into her bunny suit, zipped up the front, and continued sleeping while waiting to board her flight, and for all I know, she slept through the whole experience. Not even a twitch of an imaginary whisker. I was so envious, even after our arrival in New York, to watch her metaphorically hop through the airport off to her warren.

I know, I know, the early bird catches the worm, but as I have never knowingly eaten a worm, intentionally or otherwise, that information is low on my list of important facts to read, mark, learn, and inwardly digest, especially the worm part.

I am certainly not urging any of my peers to turn into slugabeds, but just allow *me* my eight hours before asking my brain to do anything more momentous than eat breakfast in the morning.

Just who are these masochistic people who are beating down the doors of local fitness emporiums at 5:00 a.m.? What are they thinking? The most exercise I can manage before breakfast is the opening of my eyes, and the difficult art of lifting my head from the pillow. Trust me—that is a challenge before five in the morning.

I made a semiconscious decision to join a local community group soon after my arrival in the United States. "We meet at seven thirty," a friend told me. That seemed fine to me, and I dutifully signed on the dotted line to meet every other Friday at what seemed a perfectly respectable time. I was imagining friendly suppers and stimulating after-dinner conversations, maybe followed by a convivial glass of vintage port to show them that they were not dealing with a transatlantic hippie. I should have realized that what my friend had omitted to tell me was that these meetings were breakfast meetings. *Still, not too early,* I told myself, frantically trying to justify getting up at maybe seven. Not great, but manageable. Silly me! I should have factored in the one-hour commute from my house to the meeting place, and preceding that with the minimum thirty minutes required to shrug off my jammies, get dressed, and try to locate my car in the garage with my eyes still shut.

This drive is usually spent trying to think up ways in which I can inflict pain on my hitherto friend, and how I can possibly wriggle out of this fix without appearing to be a right numpty (a delightful Scottish term for someone who is maybe not quite in total possession of all their faculties).

A battle with my conscience has ended with me telling myself to get over myself, pull up my big girl panties, stop complaining, and get on with it. As a result, I remain a member of said group— still trekking over the causeway into the big city and still grousing for a few minutes when the alarm shatters the peace of the bedroom every other Friday at zero-dark-hundred.

I have since learned to be very careful when making appointments, so please—if you want me to be coherent, with a relatively pleasant attitude, just let me wait until most normal humans are up and at 'em. Or at least until the sun is up. Yawn!

Getting Old Is Not for Sissies!

So I am no longer in the first flush of youth. In fact, I'm having trouble remembering anything remotely connected with those first flushes. In my foggy past, I seem to remember being dimly aware of awkwardness being one of my major concerns. Spots and pimples were very evident during puberty, whereas elegance and complete self-confidence surfaced quite a few years later. Who am I kidding! I'm still waiting for the elegance part, but when one is still very dependent on one's parents, one has to make up for that failing in other ways. Joining the school drama club helped, even if I did only get the character parts.

Having sailed through the sea of life, weathered a few storms, and tried to eradicate signs of the aforementioned storms on my face, I have reached the comfortable age where I really don't have to worry about how I am viewed by my peers. However, I do feel that it is totally unfair for the inner workings of one's body to start to complain bitterly when subjected to mild exercise. This happens overnight—really, it does. A couple of years ago I decided to take myself in hand. Well, nobody else wanted to do it, so I girded my loins, shook the proverbial age dust off my feet, and set about documenting what in the name of all that's limber was happening to me.

First was the eyesight. A previous twenty/twenty vision has now been adjusted more times than my bank balance. A word of warning—you have now entered the bottomless money pit of the optical shops. You may have only changed your vision specifications by a hair, but this will exponentially affect the cost. Resist the cute pair of glasses with sparkly bits, or the color-coordinated frames, because this is the downward slope to you know where.

Teeth are again a nuisance. When they're young and sparkly, they are an asset to all, and as they age, they just hurt. We wire them, bleach them, straighten and even remove them to replace them, but they are still a nuisance.

I'm not even going to mention the hair. The art of tossing one's thick and glossy locks in the breeze, whether blond or brunette (or both if that's your thing) is relegated to patting the silver or sandy hues associated with age and wisdom. Repeat after me: age and wisdom!

The cute braids or stubborn curls may well be a thing of the past. Some of us are merely trying to keep our scalp covered. Why, oh why did hats go out of fashion?

Having dealt with the top end of the body, we descend to the neck and arms. All this extra skin suddenly appears and for no good reason that I can see. As we progress south there are areas that shall remain private, even though there are more of these areas than before. This is because the real fiend is the inner workings of the human body.

Why is it that a simple task such as playing on the floor with the grandchildren has become a major event? I now have to plan the gentle crumple to the floor and hope no one is around to see the comical attempt to return to the upright stance. Leave us not discuss weeding. The spirit is willing but the flesh is weak. After thirty minutes of very light weeding, I thought nothing of it. The next morning, my quads were screaming, I was screaming, and I dare say the weeds were screaming—with laughter. Most fitness coaches will say that one has to condition oneself before indulging in any *new* activity. At the rate I'm going, putting one foot in front of the other needs to be up there on the scale of unnecessary activity, assuming that the major activity to occupy my thoughts should be breathing.

One is caught between the rock and the proverbial hard place. If inactivity is one's bag, then feel free to quietly wither away. If, like me, you feel the urge to be up and at 'em, you will pay dearly. You will have aches in places hitherto unknown to your body. To add insult to potential injury, if you start just sitting in your chair for a few months or so, when you *do* get galvanized into action, your body will leave you in no doubt of its distress—maybe not straightaway, but give it twenty-four hours.

Been there, didn't like it then, probably going again because I apparently never learn.

Driving Us Crazy!

o not shoot the messenger! I am completely unbiased on the subject of male versus female drivers. However, I have noticed that there are some traits that are gender specific. For those readers who are going to take this article way too personally, skip it and go to the next chapter.

I consider myself to be an average driver, better than some and yet not qualified for a Grand Prix trial. I was rudely brought down to earth many years ago while I was ferrying my young son to some appointment or other, and silly me, I chose this moment to ask my son and heir which parent was the better driver.

To my chagrin, he replied without any hesitation, "Daddy, because he can drive and spit out of the window at the same time."

Having that fact of life explained to me made me look at some of the weirder habits of both men *and* women when they are behind the wheel.

I'm starting with men because I'm writing this, they are not, and they'll get their chance in a page or two. It has been my observation, during my fifty years of driving in Jolly Old on the left side (or to some, the wrong side) and in the United States on the other side, that men have one driving ambition (no pun intended). They have to get the vehicle moving as quickly as possible. Doesn't matter if it's a car, a motorcycle, a boat, or maybe even a plane, it has to be started and moving immediately, and at an acceptable speed. Then, and only then, will they start to make all the adjustments that I would have been happier completing before the car was in motion. Mirrors will be adjusted, the correct radio station will be selected, to be followed by the heating, ventilation, seat positions, etc. I have never understood how men have the uncanny ability to see the world through a tiny spy hole in the yet-to-be-defrosted windscreen, but they manage it and usually reach their destination before the screen is totally clear. However, one of the best qualities that almost all male drivers have is the uncanny ability to hear a fault in the engine above the local radio and general traffic noise. What's really scary is that, having diagnosed the source of the problem, they will have it fixed before the journey is over. Kudos where it's due, I say.

Most men would rather walk than be a passenger in a car driven by the female of the species, unless she has been elected as the designated driver, and then all bets are off. Having seen some of the antics that some women get up to when behind the wheel, you cannot blame the men for choosing to walk. I have actually seen a member of the fairer sex get into her car looking as if she had just got out of bed and arrive at her destination perfectly made up, hair coiffed, and nails polished, having made all her appointments during the drive. She may not be able to hear the knocking and wheezing of a distressed engine, but throw a child into the equation, and every move or sound made by the child will be monitored closely. Threats of dire consequences will be held over the child's head unless he or she sits there buckled into the car seat and imitates a *plushie* for the duration of the ride.

Let me squash the theory that women are hopeless at changing tires. No, no, no! It's one of our best-kept secrets. Most of us are quite capable of changing tires on everything from wheelbarrows to Boeing 707s, but why should we? It's a time when men can be at their most masculine, and we women owe it to ourselves and to them to foster that approach. It's a win/win situation. The tire gets changed, we keep our manicures intact, and in addition, we have bolstered the ego of the tire changer. What's not to like?

There is one irritating trait that most of the fairer sex have, and that's the ability to talk their way out of a traffic ticket. I have seen a woman driver who was pulled over for speeding in a cemetery charm her way out of that predicament, while her male counterpart was getting the proverbial book thrown at him for just looking at a parking spot that was designated for someone else.

Let's face it—there is room for both male *and* female drivers in this world. It's just not in the same car at the same time.

A Weekend Away

The next time one of your nearest and dearest has the bright idea for the whole family to get away for the weekend, it may behoove you to dig out this checklist, or should I say warning list.

1. However much you plan ahead, there will never be enough time to pack all the correct clothes, food, and entertainment materials for each family member.
2. Count the number of children under the age of ten. This is very important as arriving at the destination with less than the number with which you left can cause distress among some members of the family. Also, the number of stops on the way is often in inverse proportion to the number of small children who started the journey with you.
3. When a small person insists that they can swim like a fish, never believe him or her unless he or she can produce ample certification, or you have actually observed said child swimming in an Olympic trial. You can choose to believe the child's claim to aqua proficiency if you are prepared to jump into an icy cold torrent, lake, or pool to retrieve said child who appears to be turning blue from the lips down.

4. Not all vegetation that is pretty and/or green may be picked or eaten. If the offending picker or eater starts to display other than a robust constitution, hose them down rapidly, coat them with a liberal layer of antihistamine, and check on the proximity of the nearest emergency station.

5. Wild creatures are, guess what? Wild creatures! They do not belong, nor do they like to be, inside the vehicle or tethered to the porch of whichever enchanting log cabin you have secured for the weekend. They certainly do not belong inside the sleeping quarters no matter how cute and cuddly they may appear. Baby versions of such animals may appear to be orphans, but I doubt whether the animal's mother will be satisfied with any excuse you can come up with as to why her baby has been summarily removed from her protection.

6. The phrase, "It's just over this next hill" offered to a novice group of hikers should be translated as, "It's a good couple of hours trek, so plan to be picked up before exhaustion sets in."

7. Secluded log cabins up in the mountains are fantastic for romantic weekends, an escape from the hectic lifestyle that most of us have to endure during the year, and a time to put your cell phones on silent for a few days. However, plan accordingly by pinpointing the location of the nearest gas station. It doesn't hurt to know exactly how far the nearest grocery store is either. One's equanimity can be shattered because while the bottle of gin may be right there in one's supply basket, if the tonic water and/or lemons are still back in the city, that does not bode well.

8. The tranquility and peace of mind that is part of a getaway weekend has to be experienced to be believed. Sitting on the porch in the evening watching the fireflies dancing and lighting up the area is not to be missed. One small problem

is that they provide an illuminated path for all the starving mosquitoes in the area on a warm summer evening. That's why smarter visitors pack enough insect repellent and antihistamine cream to stock a small pharmacy.

9. To get the most out of a weekend away, it really helps to leave the mobile phones, Xboxes, tablets, and laptops back in the big city. For a start, the reception up there in the mountains is very limited, if any. If you want to spend your weekend hanging from the roof trying for at least one or two bars on your phone, then maybe you should consider staying at home. It will stop your blood pressure from spiking, and then maybe your other guests will relax for a day or three. So be adventurous, forget the electronics, and maybe try the old-fashioned way of communication. It's called talking to each other. How novel is that? Ignore your alarm clocks and watches and wake up when it's light. Using the same logic, go to bed when it's dark. That system worked for centuries before we all became slaves to the twenty-four-hour clock.

10. When you return to the busy life from which you hopefully escaped, there is nothing that will lose you a friend more quickly than your description of your own incredible tranquil weekend away—especially when you relate this to your bosom buddy who has spent the weekend having to entertain six toddlers at a birthday party that should have been held outside in a bouncy house but due to inclement weather, they have been locked up inside a small house for humans and have had to use up all that pent-up energy by consuming cupcakes and ice cream.
Pick your moment, or better still, next time take your friend away with you.

11. For your return to the chaotic world of life in general, make sure that you return with the same number of children you

packed in the car for the outward escape. Having to drive back to your cabin to pick up a child you had encased in a straitjacket for your safety, not theirs, will not earn you any bonus points with the rest of the travelers. Plus, it increases exponentially the wails of "Are we home yet?"

12. Plan a return to the getaway location sooner rather than later to retrieve all the items that you forgot to repack for the homeward journey.

The human memory is a wonderful thing. Within a couple of months, you will have forgotten all the pain and anguish associated with the recent trip, and you will plan the next one. Will we never learn!

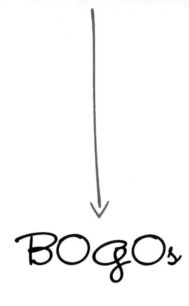

BOGOs

*D*oes anyone else out there have the same reaction to these "buy one/get one" sales methods? As I see it, stores don't do this because of their love for their fellow man but rather because they overbought on a couple of products—or half the store in many cases—and they need to get rid of these items before the sell-by date, which is another particular problem I have with this technique.

I am as gullible as the next person, and I will be one of the first in that store to load up on twenty boxes of cereal, ten of which are free, and stagger home with a self-satisfied smirk. The fact that nobody in my household even eats that particular brand is not the point. "It's free," I snarl, "so load up your cereal bowl and stop complaining that it tastes like yesterday's cardboard." To be frank, it's an infectious disease. The BOGOs await you as soon as you set foot in your usual grocery store. No matter that you just stopped in to buy some tea and a gallon of bleach. There, to tempt you, are the daily BOGOs.

For the more mathematically inclined, the stores have upped their game. No longer a BOGO—now you will see a "Buy two get the third one free," and it gets worse. Take a calculator, because the other catch is "Buy one get the second one 50 percent off." If you are without a math degree, or do not have at least a passing grade in math, you are at risk.

I would be more inclined to stop acting like one of the starving millions in the world if the stores just lowered their prices, but I suppose that they do not learn this in store-stocking school. One of these days I will cautiously creep into the local store, and they will have all of my favorite brands at rock-bottom prices with no mathematical calculation required before my decision is made. These days nothing is easy. We have been brought up to expect that if one buys a tiny packet of whatever, one would then expect the larger packet to be cheaper, right? Bulk buying? It ain't necessarily so, as the song goes, my friend. Dig out your magnifying glass (unless you have eagle eyes) and check the price per single unit. You may be surprised. Or annoyed … depending on your mood at that point in time.

As if this ploy isn't enough to lure you in, there are the dreaded coupons. No longer do you read the newspaper for news. How twentieth century is that? You get alerts on your phone instead. Today's modern shopper will spend hours with scissors cutting out a myriad of coupons for items that would not find a place in their house if they were acting rationally.

The worst part is to be caught standing in line at the checkout counter behind an avid coupon clipper. (That's the official term, or so I'm told.) This shopper will have two of the infamous shopping carts fully loaded, attached to a filing cabinet on wheels that is full of clipped, filed, and itemized coupons that have to be scrutinized independently for validity before allowing a whole five cents to be deducted from the price of a particular item. This adds about two hours to the length of time other shoppers—me in particular— have to wait before trying to get out of the store with a quart of milk before its shelf life expires.

Why is it that coupons are always for a product that wouldn't normally grace my table or frankly, my house? However, the lure is there, and given half a chance, I will swallow it hook, line, and sinker. Basically, I'm jealous. I wish I had the time, energy, but most of all the motivation to clip coupons, but I also know my own shortcomings.

Let there be a coupon for, say, puppy food, and I will collect as many coupons as I can before attempting to buy the store's entire stock of this item. I might be seen rescuing the coupon ads from waste bins throughout the county given half a chance. I may well have clipped my way into saving two dollars, but I will have a smug smile on my face as I load thirty cans of said puppy food into my cart. Do I have hungry puppies at home? Nope! Nary a one; but if I did, I would have saved two dollars.

Baby Talk!

Most grandmothers have found themselves in this position. Our presence is requested as babysitters extraordinaire while the parents take a couple of hours off. I must now list the following false statements that you will be force fed as soon as you get to the house wherein the little angels abide.

1. Don't worry, they will already be asleep when you get there.
2. If either (or all) wake up, a quick diaper change and a soothing back rub will quickly send them back to the land of nod.
3. We are just a phone call away.
4. If the oldest one toddles out of his or her room and is not a happy bunny to find out that the beloved parents are not there, just tell them to go back to bed and Mommy/Daddy will be in to see them when they get home.
5. There is no need to give them anything to eat or drink—especially in bed.
6. The TV remote is right there and is so easy to navigate.
7. There are no crayons or markers allowed in the bedroom.

8. Should one or more still be awake, they are not allowed to watch *The Walking Dead* or any other similar program.
9. They are big enough to walk; there is no need to carry them everywhere.
10. They are very tired, so there is no need for general conversation.

How easy is all this? These are my grandchildren, right? I don't need a "Granny Don't" list, I thought to myself. This just goes to show how terribly wrong even the best grandmothers in the world can be.

Let us address these rules. Any child worth its weight in diapers and Cheerios will stay awake when they hear that the parents are going out to enjoy themselves, leaving the little ones behind. No amount of explaining will convince them that they have *not* been abandoned for life. That will use up at least thirty minutes of tearful wails for "Mommeeeee" that is guaranteed to wake the smaller child, who had forgotten that the grandmother was in loco parentis for the evening. Then the fun really starts. Most younger children are really parrots dressed up as normal toddlers, so if the older one is wailing, the second one will join in, only louder. The difficulty is that whereas one has a fighting chance of understanding an almost four-year-old in between hiccups, sniffles, and threats of up chucking everywhere, with a toddler whose main purpose in life is to copy the older sibling, this becomes very hit and miss, I can tell you.

If by some miracle they are asleep when you arrive, the sound of the car door closing is enough to wake up the dead apparently. It certainly acts as an alarm to wake two toddlers.

After visits to the bathroom and diaper changes, I may be forgiven for my skeptical look when the older child told me with a perfectly straight face that backs needed to be rubbed for twenty-five minutes—'cause that's what Mommy does. Er … I don't think so, child. Nice try.

The parents may be a phone call away *if* they are in an area where there is phone reception. These so-called flat spots are only important when demented grandmothers are frantically trying to contact a parent who may well remember if all the coloring markers had their tops on when the parents left, and why does one child have a rainbow-colored tongue? The no eating and drinking rule does not apply to felt tip markers, as I have discovered, to my horror. I am so glad I'm not doing laundry in *that* house tomorrow.

Let us assume (excuse hysterical laughter) that the little cherubs are now asleep, having ingested a varied diet of fuzz-covered Cheerios, a few markers, and something that vaguely resembles an elastic hair band—the exhausted watcher may try to catch a few minutes of whatever is offered on the TV.

Please—and I cannot stress this enough—ensure that you have studied and obtained a passing grade on the how to switch on, change channels, and turn off the unfamiliar TV with the variety of remotes that are apparently in constant use.

There is no need for anyone reading this to go and tattle on me just because I had to creep into the older child's room, wake them up, and get them to operate the remote. Then you will have to start all over again getting that child back to bed—with the inevitable trip to the bathroom, and this time a much longer back rub.

Twenty-five minutes seems a fair return for me to get about three minutes of TV time, but by then the younger one will have woken up, feeling very much left out of the obvious entertaining activity that has been going on, so a repeat performance of the back rub will become the next item on the agenda.

A little later, as the sound of car doors announce the arrival home of the parents, and when asked if everything went well, you will be smart if you lie through your teeth until you have made your get-a-way. That is the time to leave the area, the neighborhood, and probably the country before the evidence comes to light, hopefully not until the following day. Children have a magical digestive system, and the inevitable bathroom visits the next day will reveal all the missing objects. Again, a word of caution. If any or both children attend a day care center, it might behoove the dropper offer to alert the staff not to freak out should any violently colored incidents come to the fore—or rather to the aft.

Why is it that we know all these things, but when asked if we would babysit again sometime in the future, we will smile and say, "I would love to."

I must remind myself to write these instructions down.

Communication!

I am reliably told that in this modern age of technology, you can get your computer to do just about anything *if* you a) have the right app or program and b) know how to use it.

Well, I obviously don't have either the right equipment installed on my methods of communication, or the skills required.

There is nothing more irritating than trying to use your elder brain with your older fingers to try to find out some information from your computer. It is very ready to tell me what I have done wrong, but that never seems to get the wretched desktop, laptop, or phone to do what I require. Frustration is rampant in my house, usually preceded by some snarky electronic voice informing me that I should be reinstalling a device driver that can be found by switching the whole thing off and then restarting the system. That cures a lot of ills. Otherwise you can turn your whole system over to a magic cursor. Admittedly, the cursor is being activated remotely by some whiz kid in outer Mongolia or somewhere just as exotic, and it is fascinating. I sat in my office one evening entranced by the fact that this brilliant technician had remotely taken charge and his/her little cursor was working like a beaver, or Mongolian equivalent, scurrying all over the place, changing screens, installing stuff, uninstalling more stuff, and generally tidying up what was my life according to computers.

What sort of life do they lead, these clever but remote operators? How depressing must it be to have to constantly deal with computer illiterates such as me? When I talk to my likeminded friends, it's just the same. They are wedded to the help line. Not a day goes by that I don't feel as if I am so unworthy to even have a computer in my house. I often wonder if the helpers all sit in their foreign countries waiting for the inevitable chat line to open up so they can try to talk some sense into operators such as myself, and then running outside to howl at the moon before returning to the inevitable tedious grind of coaxing the owner of the apparatus through a few simple steps. It must be so difficult for them to resist the urge to scream down the phone line, or whatever method the customer is using, "Switch everything off, as you have no idea what you're doing!"

I actually have some local friends who purport to know how to fix the glitches that usually I have caused myself, but even their patience wears thin after a while. I know this because lately they never answer the phone. I've got them sussed out, I can tell you. Their time will come. Probably when the current inhabitants of this earth rise up as a body, throw away all the electronic gadgetry, and revert back to writing letters. Not only would that improve our writing skills, but our reading skills would be right up there too.

Till then I am going to have to learn some more about drivers—the computer program type, not those in taxis. Shame, really. My experience with taxi drivers is much better than with the mystical creatures with exotic accents locked into the computer help programs.

I know, when all else fails, I'm calling my granddaughter. She doesn't judge me, and she has a pretty good chance of getting me back up and running. Her fee is pretty reasonable too. Guess I'll just get those cookies baked now.

Hair Today, Gone Tomorrow!

Why is it that our crowning glory, or should I say our hair, is so often the source of great exasperation during our formative years, and equally during the more senior times of our lives?

I was blessed with strong hair that was daily braided into pigtails by a mother who refused to recognize that permanently raised eyebrows may just possibly have been caused by the fact that I could not lower them if I wanted to, as my hair had been pulled back so tightly. These pigtails were useful for getting my attention and for holding me captive in a stationary position should I display signs of escaping. Add to this the fact that rotten little schoolboys thought that old-fashioned ink wells in the wooden-topped school desks were just asking for pigtails to be dipped into them, and you will quickly see that my long hair was, for me, a nuisance at school. Luckily our school uniform at that time was a blue/black gymslip (look it up if this is a new word for you), so that ink splotches from pigtail ends didn't readily show. Played havoc with the laundry though!

As we age, then, the majority of us spend more money than we have sense, cutting, shaping, coloring, and straightening (or curling) our hair depending on which type of hairstyle you fancied at any one time. At the rate of a quarter of an inch a month, plus or minus a few fractions of an inch, most of our hair failures will grow out within about six months, but women especially can go through agony waiting for their former failure to be outgrown.

Maybe we should all wear caps during our more adventurous hair years so that our mistakes may be kept undercover, so to speak. Bring back hats is what I say!

There are also a few people, mainly women, who are born with thick hair that rapidly turns into rich, cascading waves of the most magnificent mane that has ever graced a human head. The rest of the human race hates them on sight. They never have a bad hair day, and they manage to look perfectly groomed straight out of the bedroom. It just isn't fair. As my own hair is gradually turning a darkish silver (well, that's what I say on my passport and other documents), I find that now I have other hirsute problems. We all know that anno domini has a particularly nasty habit of moving the goal posts, to coin a phrase, and unfortunately, hair follicles start to get their act together in regions that you would really like left alone, thank you very much. Weird sprouts appear overnight and wave greetings at you from your reflection in the bathroom mirror. It is absolutely amazing that within the space of an overnight sleep, there will be a besprouted face looking back at you in the morning, and even while you are frantically searching for tweezers, the said sprout elongates. How dare it?

Luckily, these days there are methods of dealing with this problem. When the tweezers fail to accomplish their job, then hie yourself off to a salon where, for a ridiculous amount of money, some angel of mercy will remove such hairs and will also point out that there are other areas that need the touch of an angel sporting hot wax. It is a rather ignominious situation to be found in, relaxing on a bed while said angel puts sticks with hot waxed ends into one's nostrils just in case there are some areas that need attention. The next few seconds after the wax has set need no graphic description, but suffice it to say that *ouch* is one of the more commonly and gently used expletives. To say that one may emerge from this experience resembling a billiard ball is no exaggeration, but the shame of it is that in a few weeks the experience has to be repeated. As there may be children of tender years who may feel the urge to read this story, I will not divulge the other areas where age is accompanied by a downward drift together with the emergence of the strongest, wiriest hair growth that appears where no hair has gone before. There are things that only need to be understood with age and much wisdom and a lot of wax. As one becomes quite chatty with the wax angel, one learns that one can ask for a design when having hair removed. I kid you not! Who knew? I want to know how these angels conduct their training! Do they ask for models with hairy nostrils, armpits, and other, ahem, areas for practice sessions? How then do you describe your job? "I'm a professional model who grows hair in all the wrong places." Just a minute—isn't that the title of a song?

I have heard that there are men who are dissatisfied with the state of the nation and who will actively seek out the wax angel to remove their chest hair! They are beaten souls when they emerge, for they know that to keep the look, they will have to go back again and again!

Now if the removed hair could only be stuck to the thinning parts of our scalps. Maybe there could be a potential market if we could get the wax off the ends before applying the hair to some balding head somewhere. Hmmmmmmm. Waste not, want not, as my mother often said, but I'm pretty sure she was not thinking of recycling hair. So "hair today and gone tomorrow" will remain part of my creed for now.

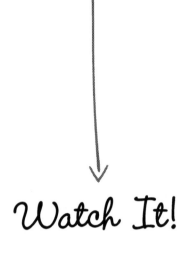

Watch It!

*W*hen I retired from the job that actually paid me a salary, to continue doing all the other jobs that didn't, and still don't, I made the conscious decision not to wear a watch anymore. Feeling quite smug with myself, I reconciled myself to this decision by analyzing my daily duties.

So here I go:

1. I will no longer be bound to the alarm clock that used to prevent me being late for work, because I don't go to work anymore.
2. I always have plenty of time to get to any appointments.
3. If I take longer than usual to prepare, order, eat, or digest my lunch, there will be no one to give me the evil eye as I return to my place of paid employment. Paid is the operative term here.
4. If I miss a bus, train, or plane, I can always catch the next one.
5. If I miss a hair appointment, I am unlikely to be banned from the conference room in case I scare the other attendees.
6. I will always have plenty of time to do the mundane but necessary chores in my life, such as preparing my tax return. (Just who am I kidding?)

7. I will make out timely shopping lists so I am adequately prepared for my planned entertaining, to include feeding other members of the household—and that's entertaining all by itself, let me tell you.

8. I will schedule visits from contractors so that I have plenty of free time to prepare for the invasion.

9. When I have ordered an item, and I am told that it will be delivered between the hours of sunrise and sunset, this will fit neatly into my ordered life.

10. I will be able to saunter up to the appropriate school building where one of my grandchildren is patiently waiting to be collected because I have loads of time and who needs a watch anyway!

So who can see the flaws in all of the above statements? Let me describe how the very decision to go watchless was a mental aberration on my part that may have scarred me for life.

1. If I do *not* set the alarm in the morning, there is a 90 percent chance that I will be roused from my slumber by a phone that is ringing off the hook (and I'm sorry, I can tell by the agitated ring that it is my daughter) to remind me that I promised to be wherever I had foolishly agreed to meet hours ago, and now everyone is late and of course it's all my fault. The remaining 10 percent chance is that I will be summoned from my bed somewhat dishabille because there is someone banging at the door.

2. I do make plans to get to my appointments on time, but little things distract me, such as not remembering where I put the directions to said appointee, or just chatting too long with the mail lady, or just pick an excuse. The one medical office that will get me there not only on time, but usually early, is the office that told me when I signed up that

my doctor didn't tolerate tardiness—one had a five-minute grace period, and then you would need to reschedule. I did wonder why there were patients camping outside the office. Now I know. I may have to join them in future as I barely made the last appointment. I arrived to the office out of breath, wearing odd shoes, and I do believe I had breakfast cereal liberally scattered on my shirt.

3. Lunches I have always thought of as being the ultimate date. One sashays in with manicured nails, elegantly shod feet, and perfectly coiffed hair so that one can take all the time in the world to select, nibble, drink, and return to one's ordered life. Triple wrong. There is a critical time window so that harassed servers can remember you and your order and get you in, fed, and out of there so that the next worried group can take your place. Beware being late for *that* appointment, because you will go very hungry.

4. Missing scheduled forms of transportation is just another form of hell. Of course you can be rebooked on another flight, madam—for a fat fee. By the way, there is no other direct flight until tomorrow. That'll teach you to get there on time.

5. Missing beauty appointments is a huge no-no. When one is retired, there is a tendency to let things slip. (No pun intended!) Read, mark, learn, and inwardly digest these words. Whatever else you give up, visits to the beauty salon should never be one of them. We are all having to deal with Mother Nature and gravity, not necessarily in that order, which is hard enough without giving them a free ticket to experiment.

6. Never, never put off doing your tax return—unless you are married to a millionaire who has his own accountant. It will give you sleepless nights, and cause you to slink around like a criminal. Face facts! Births, deaths, and taxes need to be taken care of. So pull up your big girl panties and get

'em done. Unless the millionaire is a factor. Does he want
to adopt me?

7. Shopping is another fact of life, and the longer you delay,
    the more fast foods you will imbibe and the more inches
    you will acquire, and the result is that you will be fatter
    and grumpier.

8. Remember that you are employing contractors. If you have
    failed to prepare for their invasion, they will charge you
    for wasted time, because they don't care—money is money.
    So plan ahead, set the clock, and smile sweetly as the dust
    settles on your head.

9. Don't you hate this delivery time when you have no idea
    when it/they will arrive? As I have yet to be the first drop-
    off I can only assume that they don't work in the mornings
    at all, and just double up on time between five and six p.m.
    Now there's someone who doesn't set his or her clock.

10. Anyone who has arrived late to pick up a traumatized
    child from a school or equivalent will know the feeling
    of abject shame as one slinks into the building to hear
    sobbing child in the background hiccupping, "I thought
    you'd forgotten me ..."

Add to that the stony glares of the teachers as one creeps in,
head down, whispering sorry to anyone who even dares to make
eye contact, and one will never, ever be late again, barring death
or dismemberment.

So my point is that you may not have to be at a place of work at
a certain time each day, but our lives are governed by our watches,
whether we like it or not, so don't try to tell yourself you can throw
away your watch, because we all know you have your cell phone
with you with the time and date right there on the front. Tempus
fugit, whether you watch it or not, so you might as well try to be
on time.

Put a Sock in It!

I'm not really a believer in ghosties and ghoulies and things that go bump in the night, but believe me, there is a being that lives in my house who (or which) is determined to upset my equilibrium.

This thing, whom I shall dub Francis, for no other reason other than I don't personally know anyone of that name who might take umbrage, is causing me more than a little bother.

Francis is the being that taunts me every time I do laundry. I'm sure you all have a Francis living with you. It's Francis who knots the sheets in the washer, sneaks a pair of red unmentionables in with the whites, and steals a sock every chance he or she gets. I'm favoring the he type of Francis because that type of sick humor seems to be of the male persuasion, rather like a mischievous schoolboy. Back to the socks, or lack of.

I have tried counting them carefully, placing them inside a string bag, and tying it up. I can attest to the fact that nobody else goes into my laundry room—except Francis. Why would they? Once you're in there, you had better do something useful, such as a load of laundry.

After the wash cycle, I remove the string bag—still closed up, you understand—and then I untangle the towels (heaven forbid they should retain their shape) and place all the wet laundry into the dryer. Now is the time when Francis comes into his own. First, he will make the knot on the string sock bag so tight that it's impossible to undo without the loss of several fingernails, but beforehand he will remove a number of socks and hide them. This is the critical part. He manages to hide them in places that are unknown to me or to anyone else living in this house. However, he never hides a pair of socks. This is the diabolical reasoning that makes me think Francis is not of this earth—if he hid a matched pair, one might think that in the heat of the moment, one had forgotten to wash that particular pair. Oh no! It's only ever one of a pair that is spirited away, never to be seen again until many weeks—even months—later, by which time the lone sock of the pair has pined away for its partner and has shriveled up, totally unwearable.

I think I may have discovered Francis's secret stash—totally by accident, you understand—because I really have better things to do with my time than go on a weekly sock hunt—and it involved my ongoing battle with duvet covers. In a weak moment, I was undergoing one-on-one instruction from my daughter on the infallible method of replacing the cover on my duvet when I found myself unable to smooth out some odd-shaped wrinkles right at the top of said cover after it had been applied, buttoned, and smoothed. Hiding these awkward bulges from my instructor, who would have made me take the whole thing off to start again, I waited until I was alone. I then unbuttoned the cover and actually crawled inside, right to the top, to find what felt like stray socks.

"Francis, you have met your match!" I muttered to myself, wriggling out to examine the cache.

To give Francis his due, there was one old (but clean) sock, for which the matching item had been long since discarded, but to my horror, the sock was wrapped around a very scanty thong—and I do *not* mean the type that one wears on one's feet. It was *not* mine, because I was never that small, even at birth, and they were of a color that only sees light of day in my house when the house occupants are very, very sick.

I have yet to find the owner, but I bet Francis knows!

Come Fly with Me!

There was a time when even the mention of airports sent me into a fantasy land that included the seven wonders of the world, hula dancers, or maybe the Christmas markets of Europe. I would plan with excitement and dress for the occasion because you never knew who might be seated next to you.

Well, that's in the past, I can tell you. I start taking the proper precautions months ahead of any scheduled flight just to keep my stress level at manageable level, because just as sure as babies fill diapers, any airline with whom I have flown will try their level best to reduce me to a gibbering mass of skin and bone—and that's before I even set foot inside the airport building.

It begins when one tries to purchase a ticket. Remember those gentle days when one would be greeted and welcomed by some honeyed voice whose only job in the whole wide world was to please you, sell you a plane ticket, and indicate to you that the entire airline would be waiting just for you at your convenience. I dimly seem to be aware of the phrase customer service, but that was *soooooooo* long ago.

To start, it really depends just how much patience you have as you will be put on hold while some irritating singsong computer tells you off because you didn't book online! Why am I embarrassed by a computer? This technology is going too far. When a highly bored operative does condescend to speak with you, it costs extra. Serves you right for not booking online. Heaven forbid you should want to check a bag. Your credit card is starting to have palpitations because your budgeted flight has already gone into overdraft. Maybe I'm just being picky, or I've chosen an airline whose staff have had their days off cut, but they do seem to derive pleasure from our discomfort. All this and it's still months before your scheduled trip. So—bring your blood pressure back to normal.

Let us assume your trip has not been cancelled or rerouted through the southern hemisphere when you only want to go from Tampa to Atlanta, for example, and let's play the game where you get to the correct airport well in time for your flight. Now it's fun time. You get to choose your seat! Yay! What you cannot find out is who will be sitting next to you. If you are small in stature, the odds are highly in your favor of you being seated next to someone who really should have the whole row of seats to themselves. Not because they may be just a little heavier than you, but because they travel in groups, and they will *all* be in your row. Happens every time. They are the nicest people who have to put their carry-on baggage in the overhead compartment, but they will need to access these bags on average every five minutes. You, being smart, will have chosen the aisle seat. Did you ever make the wrong choice? If you are under 140 pounds, go for the window seat every time. Trust me.

There are some airports that are hubs. This means that like the spoke of a wheel, the concourses radiate out from the center. Sounds logical until you are given the wrong gate information by either a harassed flight attendant, or one who has just about had it with moaning passengers and is itching to get his or her own back. Off you trot in entirely the wrong direction for *miles*, only to be told that there was, is, or will be a gate change, and of course, it's at the other end of an entirely different concourse. This, however, has its good points. If you were 140 pounds when you enplaned (love that term … bit like "Beam me up, Scotty"), by the time that you have trotted the length and breadth of the airport in question with carry-on bags that seem to be filled with wet sand, only to trot all the way back again, you will now be down to at least 135 pounds. On the flip side, your blood pressure will be spiking to apoplexy. It seems to me of late that passengers will do anything to avoid checking bags, which means that their carry-on bags are bulkier, more angled, and a real hazard to anyone who has had the misfortune to enplane earlier. If you have never had the sharp corner of a carry-on bag clout you at ear level, then you haven't traveled, my friend.

There have been times, very, very few, when I have traveled first class. Mainly because I had a surfeit of frequent flyer miles in the days when it was a use-or-lose situation. These days it is another world. Never has the void between them and us ever been flaunted to such a length. Consider first class! As soon as the great divide has been set with a flourish of the curtain, one's blood pressure sinks to normal levels, the attendants take one's jacket and hangs it up, and small glasses of a sparkling champagne are administered to put one in a proper frame of mind. No food carts in first, I might add. One is given a tray with linen cloth and real grown-up cutlery. Light banter between guest and attendant floats through the cabin, and one feels as if one has been born to this kind of travel.

On the *other* side of the curtain, attendants have a fixed grimace on their faces and push those obnoxious carts up and down the aisles with a ferocity that makes any aisle seaters shake in their shoes, slippers, or if they're smart, steel-capped shoes. Personally, I love to watch the fight for the teeny-tiny bathrooms. It is the passenger seated furthest away who has been dancing from foot to foot watching for the signal that the cubicle is free (nobody can call it a room), and while he is navigating the aisle with a nifty turn of speed, a sneaky passenger from *waaaay* up front will nip out in front, rush into the cubicle, and slam the door shut. I have since learned the art of hovering outside said cubicle door. Nobody is going to cheat me out of my turn!

When eventually one deplanes—got to love these terms—one may well have to say a few prayers while hoping that your baggage made it on to the same flight, and even more important, some kind baggage handler took it off the plane in the same airport to which you are traveling. There are a lot of possibilities here, fellow traveler, and some alternatives are quite puzzling. I have begun to notice that travelers are now starting to put weird identification markers on their bags. That's usually worth a few moments of quiet amusement, but I beg of you—don't make your studies of other people's bags too evident, or you may find that their sense of humor isn't quite on the same level, and the result may be unpleasant for the observer.

The key word for air travel, unless you are rich and can travel in the manner to which we all would like to be accustomed, is tolerance. It's not worth the aggravation, so take your time, be flexible, and come fly with me!

My House Elf!

Please don't read this title and assume that I'm piggybacking on a well-known (and by now, very rich) author. It's just that the very idea of a house elf really appeals to me and mine. I would have to be very careful not to upset the flesh-and-blood helpers that are to be found within the confines of my family, nor would I decry their patience and pitying expressions, but a house elf? Think about it.

By virtue of their very existence, house elves operate where you are not. They are unlikely to ask you to lift your feet while running a vacuum between you and your couch, nor are they about to make a quiet comment when you decide to sally forth wearing what should be described as a flour sack with a belt. Nope! House elves would usually not be seen. They will make sure that you have enough victuals in the kitchen cabinets and refrigerators so that you may astound your guests with culinary plates of goodness, but your house elf would make sure that your dishes would end up being clean and sparkly ready for your next foray into the art of gourmet cooking.

All you really have to do to keep your house elf sweet tempered is to give them a name, and be polite. Provide them with respect, and they will work for you for as long as you live in your current abode. Do not forget, house elves are attached to the respective house where they are employed, and it's just not possible to take them with you should you decide to pack up and go. I feel that house elves have a connection to the brick-and-mortar shelter where they work, and they are due a certain amount of respect.

Having said all this, I need to locate the employment agency that specializes in house elves for the more discerning homeowner. When one buys a property, a list of potential applicants for that particular house should be offered. They require little in the way of food because they are by definition faerie folk, but they are the best at keeping the household under control, as far as housework is concerned.

I am obviously going to have to resort to digging out the house sale paperwork because I think I may have failed to register for my house elf when I bought my house. By the state of the kitchen after I have had guests and the debris generally scattered about, I must have committed some elf crime, because nowhere is there evidence of a resident house elf. I have deliberately left little elf gifts on shelves and on garden seats, but they are still there the next day, having been totally ignored.

I told other members of the family that I needed a house elf, and one of them had the gall to say that they thought I *was* the house elf. Needless to say, their Christmas gift has been donated to a respectful and needy person. They are lucky that I allow them in the house after that comment. How very dare! So here is my advertisement to have a house elf restored to my property.

Wanted: House elf for a deserving homeowner. Will suit elderly elf as there are no stairs to be climbed and currently no pets or children in residence.

Children, however, are frequent visitors but tend not to stay very long—unless the cookie supply is unlimited, and then you have a hard time getting them out of the house.

All equipment for cleaning will be provided, and the selected elf will have free access to the refrigerator and food pantry.

References are required as flighty elves with a sense of mischief would fare better in a household with younger homeowners.

Still waiting!

Love Me, Love My Sloth!

I have been reading a lot of travel news lately, and the one thing that leaps to mind is the variety of service animals that one may take as a companion on a plane. The imagination boggles! Miniature horses, really? Surely they jest, but I fear not. I just want to know how the owner fits their "service" animal into the tiny closets that they call lavatories in the main cabin. Even horses have to answer the call of nature, and that is likely to be quite a considerable call during any flight longer than an hour. *Who gets to clean that up?* I ask myself. My answer is, *Not me!*

I have seen lists of other "service" creatures that include boa constrictors, peacocks, rats, pigs (the cute little ones), and goats, to name but a few. My first thought is that several of these critters, no matter how enchanting, have a powerful body perfume at the best of times, and when enclosed in an aircraft cabin, that has got to produce some pretty eye-watering aromas.

I have decided that my service animal should be a two-toed sloth. There are several very obvious advantages. The major one is that everything about this animal exudes calmness and serenity. Gone would be all the stress of screeching through the main terminal because I really don't think a sloth is capable of screeching anywhere.

I will find that my sloth and I will be soooooooo relaxed that when proceeding through customs, the agents will doze off while asking us if we have anything to declare. I can see that the slowness of our responses on board might mean that our meal choices are not the freshest, but there are very obvious advantages for a sloth and his/her companion traveler. We will always be selected to sit near agitated passengers to try to keep them calm. They will either burst a blood vessel trying to get responses from us, or they will themselves, with no coercing, join the ranks of the relaxed travelers who are a delight to have as fellow passengers.

Should the sloth be of good size, it could travel draped around one's neck and may be used as a cushion. By the time the sloth has registered concern, one will already have reached one's destination.

I really do feel that this creature has been often maligned and its qualities overlooked. When is the last time any of us have read a book that has had a sloth as the main character? See? My point entirely. I feel the time has come to bring this animal to the forefront of society, except by the time the sloth has opened its eyes, society will have moved on.

Who Are You Calling Patsy?

I am fully aware that I am a sucker for sob stories, but I am also incapable of turning away those unsolicited little people who knock on your door armed with millions of reasons why I should buy whatever it is that they are trying to offload. Selling isn't quite what they do; bullying is much more like it.

It's no good—I feel so sorry for them. When they have apparently been schlepping this box of unwantables around all day and I am the only gullible Gertie that answers the front door—what's a person to do? Some of them are so good at this I swear they have spray-on tears. Add a quivering lip, and I'm undone. I once spent an hour listening to a poor soul—really, he was so downcast because nobody would buy his box of frozen meats and he was going to lose his job if he didn't offload this last incredible offer and he could see that I was the sort of person with a nose for a bargain as well as a heart, etc. I had to be restrained.

I do believe it was my son who eventually hauled me back inside and politely told the seller that I was not allowed to buy anything at the front door as I was not permitted to handle real money anymore!

I thought that was a trifle harsh and huffily said as much to said son and heir. The response was a pitying smile, and he did ask me where I thought I was going to store this fifteen kilos of blood-festooned meat as my small freezer space was bulging already. Later that day as I had occasion to walk down the street, I remember that I was on a leash for my own protection at the time, I saw my former "poor soul" climbing into a 911 Porsche! Now what's wrong with that picture?

I really do have even more of a problem with telemarketers. They are *soooooo* polite and disarming on the phone, and before I have really figured out who wants what and how much, we are all discussing my corns, the weather in Europe, alligators in sewers, and the price of tea in China, and by the way, of course I would love for them to come and visit. I'm likely to find out down the line that in between my corns and China, I have signed up to send regular payments to the Save-A-Sloth pedicure society. By the way, have you seen the size of a sloth's toenails? They would use up a five-gallon can of nail polish in a heartbeat.

It's not just my flesh-and-blood family either. My financial adviser starts to shake his head no even before I start dialing his number. "But it's such a great deal!" is my plaintive whine to him when I have read on the back of some grubby piece of paper that the deal of the century is only open to a very select discerning few. I even try rationalizing with him that this potential transaction would otherwise be going right down the porcelain receptacle. The sad part is that he's usually right, but I feel the need to keep him on his toes. After all, if one is an adviser, one has to advise, right? Although I can really do without the sniggers, thank you very much!

The latest piece of gullibility is the social media network that not only exposes the frailty of many of the users but most certainly exposes the fact that I am not to be trusted with a keyboard and a computer. Having scrolled through some general chat (fairly harmless), my eye caught the phrase, "If you are between the age of sixty and sixty-five, you are most certainly paying double if not triple the amount of car/house/life insurance, so click here to get competitive quotes." Champing at the bit, I filled in the questionnaire, and therein lies the rub. Within seconds, and I am not exaggerating, my email inbox started to fill up and the phone started to ring.

They must have seen me coming. The only thing that could make this worse is if they called at zero-dark-hundred because then I forget my delicate upbringing and have been heard to utter such phrases as, "Get a life! Get off my phone or simply go away!" I do believe I had recourse to tell one persistent caller to bugger off, but then he did call at eight thirty one Sunday evening … really?

One of the clues to identify a telemarketer or some other form of bloody nuisance is the way in which they use your first name, many times in the same sentence. Also, a general discussion concerning your day, the weather, and life in general before they get to the point are other markers. Don't write to me and tell me that I should use caller ID, because I do, but not everyone is nice enough to provide this information, and some of my dearest friends simply haven't set that up. There's always a sneaking suspicion that if you don't answer this unrecognizable number, you will miss out on some significant news, such as you being this week's mega-millions winner. That might work if I ever bought a ticket.

So please, for my family's sanity, and my peace of mind, do not contact me asking me for money—else I am assured that there are scurrilous members of my family who are planning to hold me down and tattoo the word *no* on my forehead. As long as the rule also applies to them, I'm okay with that, but then I am the original sucker. My ventures into philanthropic activities will make me feel good about myself, but even I draw the line at buying a named brick for a bridge that I was asked to fund in the Kalahari desert. I'm no patsy! I know—I've seen my birth certificate.

O Come, All Ye Frightful!

'Tis the season when most of us try to creep into the nearest hair salon in an attempt to hide what we've become, and to be recreated as a new you or us. Don't think that it's only the female of the species either, as I have been almost personally trampled by members of the masculine gender in a race to get the last open chair in these magical emporiums. Should that be emporia if it's plural? However, you do get my gist, right? Whatever happened to, "After you, ma'am"?

Back to the subject matter, these salons manage to work miracles on most of us, allowing us to hold our heads higher when we leave, and leaving inches of split ends and peroxide disasters on the floor. I have always wanted to put a streak of color in my hair, other than the one given to me by my genes and a higher being, but I just cannot bring myself to create such a radical change. Suppose my hypothetical blond streak turned orange? Or even green. Or maybe the cute curls that looked so delightful in the magazine may end up looking as if I had a run in with several corkscrews if I actually succumbed.

I personally think that the nomenclature of these stores is all wrong in this country. "Beauty shop" is one of the names often heard bandied about, which I really think is putting a lot of pressure on the beautician. Be serious. I know beauty is in the eye of the beholder, but let's be realistic. Some of us are a lost cause before we ever make an appointment. Why is it then that the proverb "One cannot make a silk purse out of a pig's ear" comes so forcefully to mind? All most of us need is the special time spent with our favorite stylist of the moment, who will take the matted thatch on the top of our heads, clean it, trim it, color it, crimp it, tone it, and then spray the result with quick-setting concrete to perform miracles. This has the end result of disgorging from the chair a complete stranger. I think this is deliberate. Even if you don't score a ten on the beauty scale (who are we kidding … if I get to 3.5, it's magical), you will at least be totally unrecognizable as the creature that crawled in under the covers of multiple headscarves. Why do we do this? Do we hate who we are? Is our inner person any better after we've coughed up lots of money to be changed?

I think such salons ought to be called churches. I tell my stylist things that I wouldn't tell in the confessional if I was of the religious persuasion that did such things. Never mind national security! If the men in dark suits want to find out any information about any of us, they need to talk to the requisite beautician, stylist, or barber. I have sat in a chair waiting for my turn to be recreated, and due to sheer proximity, I have learned things about an adjacent client that I would hope their banker, priest, and general family members never get to hear! It's enough to make one's hair curl without artificial aid too.

I have to mention prices because it's like a fairy tale. It's sheer fantasy. Any number of my friends and acquaintances, male *and* female, will gripe about the increase in a gallon of milk, price of gas, ad nauseam, but will happily impart with many, many dollars in the hope that a newer person will emerge from the chosen salon.

We will be stony broke, as we say in the old country, but as no one will recognize us it doesn't matter.

Just think! In about six weeks or so, we can do this all over again. During that period, we will be busily turning ourselves into a chrysalis betting on the fact that a completely new person will emerge after our visit to the salon, beauty shop, or barber. I do draw the line at calling it a visit to the chop shop, because that implies that I was a complete ruin before, just needing to be detailed, and only after taking off old bits and welding on newer parts will I be ready to face the world again. No longer frightful but just no longer me, either.

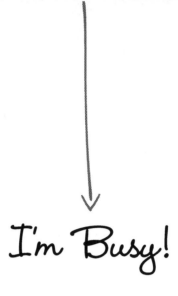

I'm Busy!

$\mathcal{J}$ust these two little words, and one's life revolves round them as one ages.

Why is it that in our younger days, even as a single working parent with two kids in school, working a full forty hours a week, taking care of the pet, helping with homework, cooking dinner, doing laundry, and belonging to a couple of clubs (No! Not the kind of club where you hope nobody will recognize you) do we still find time for our friends? As we get older, we have less to do, but we also seem to have less time available in case we even want to do anything vaguely earth shattering. Ask yourself how many times you've checked your calendar and said to yourself, "My, I'm so busy." Aye, that'll be right, as they say with raised eyebrows in bonnie Scotland.

The sad thing is that when we *do* have an engagement—quite often we forget to write it down, and then maybe, just maybe we double date ourselves.

Is this because we're *soooooo* busy? Nope! It's because we are dipsticks, and if we forget to write down the first appointment, we will manage to screw up the second appointment too.

Trust me—it doesn't work to try to cram both in, because you will not come out of this looking good. Either you will screech out of the, let's say, dental office with floss hanging out of your mouth (not a pretty picture at any time), and then when you get to your second appointment, you will have missed happy hour, or at least the free appetizers. To me that smacks of a lose/lose situation.

In an ideal world, one would have a secretary to spread out one's appointments and a Jeeves to remind one where one should be and when. If you haven't noticed, I don't have either, and as we do not live in said ideal world, we need to get a grip.

The difference between our earlier really busy lives and our currently poorly managed lives is sleep. Most of us who are of a mature age (let's say we won't be seeing twenty-one again) will remember the days when we would be oh so grateful to get six hours of uninterrupted *ZZZZZZs*, and yet today, the idea of even being coherent before nine a.m. makes me shudder. I have discovered that my usual polite and understanding personality, for which I am known, will turn into a snarling zombie like character should an unfeeling person call me at eight a.m. plus or minus an hour. Why do they always say, "Did I wake you?" when you pick up the phone? One of these days I will find the chutzpah to reply, "No, I am still asleep!" and hang up. My unfeeling family tell me to just ignore these early callers, but it's like an errant smoke alarm. That ringing will go on and on and on until someone (usually me) cracks.

So a gentle awakening at about 8:45, a discussion with my inner self as to which devastatingly impressive set of clothing I should don, a languid stroll around the bathroom wandering in and out of the shower, followed by the singularly most important part of the morning's ritual—the first cup of hot tea—and by then it is likely to be bordering on pre-lunch cocktail time. So now you can understand how busy I am.

My worst nightmare is the early morning pre-breakfast annual physical appointment that is usually at eight a.m. (They did try to schedule me for 7:30 a.m., but the hysteria that followed caused them to reschedule rapidly.) No tea, no creams or perfumes to assist me in disguising my nighttime face that takes a full hour before it falls into place, just the knowledge that I will have to stand on a set of scales that I cannot get to lie. I should confess that I did once try standing with one foot on the scales, while dangling the other off to the side in the vain hope that the scale wouldn't notice. It did. I gave it a quick kick on the way out anyway. Well, let's face it—all these happenings before I'm fully awake upsets my equanimity.

I have now discovered the art of looking busy. Walk everywhere very quickly, or as speedily as your physical self will allow, but have a clipboard under your arm. Note: Blank paper won't work. Get a list, even if it's your laundry list, but get a list and a functioning writing implement. Lipsticks don't count. People will then give you a wide berth because you look *sooooo* busy.

His and Hers!

Have you ever taken a few minutes and cursed the evolution of our species over the past thousands of years? When was the era where it was decided that men could cruise into a hair salon, barber, or unisex something or other and sit down without an appointment to get a haircut while we women have to plan months in advance? Was there a vote? If there was, I missed it.

I am continually amazed that haircuts for men take two minutes if the barber is slow, ten minutes if the barber is chatty, and forty-five minutes if the barber is called a hairstylist. Men can emerge from getting their hair cut and *never* have to suffer from bedhead, nor do they have bad hair days. Why is it when they start to show signs of gray, it's a sign of elegance and maturity, but when the women first notice evidence of fading color, it's a sign of pending wheelchairs and planning for a full-time carer.

I am not going to even touch on the subject of price because there's obviously a factor here that has escaped me. A quick trim for a man may cost him fifteen dollars unless he's conned a female acquaintance to tidy him up with a pair of hair clippers, and in that case it's free, while for us more fastidious females, a small loan may have to be planned in advance. If a man gets a rubbish haircut, in two days the hair has grown out. If a woman makes a wrong decision with a new hairstyle, it's with her for months. During this time, it is the unwritten sods law that photos will be taken and recorded for posterity, or life-changing meetings will take place all while the poor victim really wants to be pointed to the nearest wig shop.

I've made a couple of observations during my continual visits to various hair salons that are not 100 percent accurate but are just a guide. If you are kept waiting for longer than fifteen minutes, there's something wrong with the system, so be prepared for some kind of disappointment. Next, if the salon floor is strewn with various bits of hair because nobody has swept it up since breakfast the day before, I'd for sure check their hygiene regime. Now the decisive factor for me is how often the stylist looks in the mirror to primp, pat into place, comb, or pin their *own* hair while they are waving scissors around your own crowning glory. An additional factor would be if said stylist has a hairstyle that would cause bigfoot to run for his life. These stylists are too busy relating their personal problems to listen to your ideas about your own hair and are probably not going to care one way or another. Leave and try somewhere else.

As a much younger person, I used to snigger unkindly when I heard older people go into a panic mode because they were having to move to a different place and they would have to start the search for someone to cut their hair. Forget the new house, new area, and new friends. Find me someone who understands my hair.

I snigger no longer. I'm ashamed to say that I have planned a transatlantic trip around the date when I knew that my former hairstylist could give me an appointment. How sad is that? If you are ever in St. Andrews, Scotland, and need a hairstylist that won't have you walking around with your head in a paper bag, let me know. I'll give you the name of the best stylist in Fife. Trust me on this one.

Vain? Of course it is. Other than shaving your head, you are going to have to get something done to your hair sooner or later, so use it to your advantage. Guys? You're on your own. We've got enough things to worry about.

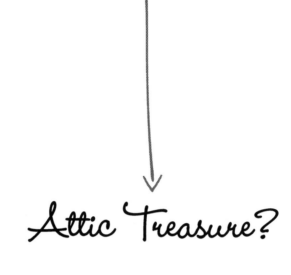

Attic Treasure?

*W*ell, one thing leads to another, and before I knew what I was getting into, I decided that there were things in my attic whose origin was suspect to say the least.

You have to realize that to even get into my attic was not so much curiosity but more a leap of faith. The fact that the scampering of tiny feet may have triggered this totally irresponsible decision on my part may have more than a grain of truth at its source is neither here nor there. I'm leaning toward the "there" in case the tiny feet manifest themselves into real live critters—with *teeth*, no less.

No matter how nimble one is, any rapid climbing up and down an attic ladder is not for the frail, not for the over forties, and definitely not for the "comfortable" in the weight area. Any one of these three criteria qualifies for a "not on your life, fella" decision. In my case, it was a very polite "after you," as a number of former friends and acquaintances made the rash decision to investigate on my behalf. I did say former friends, did I not? They appear to have become somewhat reclusive of late—hence the term *former* friends.

After a while, and after I had had contractors working up there, the scampering desisted, and I decided that the time had come. I needed the storage space, so things had to go. I do have some advice for anyone rash enough to embark on such an adventure here in Florida: *never, ever* do this during the summer. Unless you are rich enough to warrant installing air conditioning in your attic, you will last about four minutes, and that's on a cloudy day. The temperature is well over the "fry an egg on the floor" level, so choose your time well.

Having bribed a couple of friends to do my dirty work, the anticipation was electric. First on the list was an oil painting, on canvas, and tastefully framed in a very dirty but gilded frame. The canvas was held in place by cockroach casings, or whatever the entomological name is, and the actual painting was, I think, a still life of a vase of flowers. My indecision is due to the fact that most of the oil had melted, dried, and flaked off, so I'm really just guessing at the origin of the composition. The artist's name sadly rang no bells either with me or with the internet, so that find was banished to the trash. I had to guess at the signature, but Picasso and Klee fans—worry not. The rest of the finds consisted of a fake Christmas tree with just three branches—don't ask—and several boxes of just plain stuff that I had cajoled my family into cramming into the attic for now, just until I get totally unpacked. This was six years ago, so that's an indication of the importance of the items.

So, no treasures! Lots of dust and a lot of boxes that are destined for the nearest place that will take donations. Who needs four dozen additional juice glasses, TV stands that do not belong to anything in my house, a small skeleton of some desiccated critter, and enough Christmas lights to illuminate any multistory building in the area?

On a good note, some of the space is now floored, so I have tons of room to store all the things that I was going to donate—with the exception of the three-branched Christmas tree. In the future, who knows, there could be a run on juice glasses and my attic treasures will be in demand, especially if you need a Christmas tree obviously missing three branches. I hope I remembered to take a head count of the people who had nothing better to do than crawl up into my attic as it has been an exceptionally hot summer. Anyone missing a family member?

Next, I may begin to clean out the garage. After all, there's space in the attic.

Tripping the Light Fantastic!

How *times have changed*, said everybody at some time or other during their span on this earth. Any venture onto a social media network will see little quizzes labeled, "Do you remember when?" which is a young person's concession to the fact that some of us who are pre-pre-millennials may actually have had a life back in olden times, and what's more, we enjoyed most of it too.

Apart from the obvious changes in fashion wear, there is one enjoyment that is a rarity these days but that was a requirement if you ever wanted to make an impression on a member of the opposite sex. You had to know how to dance. You didn't need to be a Nureyev, or a Margot Fonteyn, but you did need to be able to tell the difference between a waltz and a quickstep if you wanted to make headway with your intended. I have been reliably informed that standing on your partner's toes and letting them do all the work was never and never will be the solution to your own lacking in the terpsichorean area.

I have often wondered where the phrase "Tripping the light fantastic" comes from, and I do believe I now know. Tripping is what happens when you fail to respond to your partner's body language and tread heavily on his or her toes. The fantastic part is when you watch a pair of dancers floating round the ballroom in perfect synchronization. They appear to be welded together, and every part of their body is finely tuned to the music and faint pressure of their partner's hips, which hopefully will give you all the required information. Contrast these movements with those of a couple whose objective may be the same, but whose execution should be just that—an execution.

Why, oh why, can't that person convey to their feet that the waltz beat should be a one, two, three and that in no way can you get a count of four to fit.

The couples who start the dance as a wrestling match are quite entertaining to watch to see who is going to be the winner, and actually lead their partner. When it's the female of the species who ends up victorious, her partner will usually last through the dance and then make a judicious beeline for the bar—to exert his masculinity, no doubt.

Personally, I miss the old style dance halls where young ladies could get a group of like-minded friends and sit and giggle together in a corner waiting to be asked to dance. It wasn't always necessary to have an escort. In fact, it was better to go as a freelance group. The theory was quite sound. Your usual escort may well be great company but a really rotten dancer, but if you go to a dance as a group, you stand a good chance of being asked to dance by a variety of different partners. The plus side is that most often 50 percent would be fairly competent. If they were rubbish, then after your obligatory three minutes of dance time, you could return to your group—bloody but unbowed. Potential partners also learned quickly that the belle of the ball was not always the best choice of dance partner as she would usually be surrounded by candidates for Prince Charming, leaving the rest of the field clear for us lesser mortals.

So where do modern youth trip the light fantastic these days? Do they buy tickets for rock concerts and spend their time ecstatically trying to dislocate their necks and upper body parts? Do most of them even know that there are dance floors where, in days long gone now, we antiquarians would astound the masses with our ease and fluidity at the foxtrot, quickstep, and waltz? Those more daring would attempt the tango or even the cha-cha. Our dresses of multiple frothy layers of chiffon and silk would sparkle with millions of sequins and dazzle the opposition, but a word of caution: the heels on our dance shoes were usually so high that any careless movement was likely to end in disaster.

I'm somewhat ashamed (but secretly proud) to remember a time when I and my dance partner for that evening were tripping our own light fantastic during the performance of a very elaborate rendition of the quickstep, and giving a credible account of ourselves too. However, a taller and much heavier couple decided to give us our comeuppance by executing an unsignalled change of direction, resulting in an elbow block that rocked us back on our heels.

After we had recovered, the gauntlet was taken up. A judicious thrust of my partner's hips indicated that I should be ready, and on his whispered command of "now," I stepped back smartly with my five-inch spiked heels and impaled the opposition through the cuff on his pants, pinning him to the floor. The moral to this story is if you are going to trip the light fantastic, don't bully the opposition, and don't wear pants with cuffs.

Bigger and Better Spiders!

In this day and age, one has to weigh the good against the bad and make the appropriate choice. Take Florida! On the good side, there's sunshine for most days of the year, when it *does* rain, it doesn't mess about, and there will be no doubt in your mind that it is raining. It may not last long, but one will get more than a trifle damp if one hovers outside for longer than five minutes.

Moving right along, there are the critters! This varies from the cute lizard-like geckos (I've yet to know the difference) to things with very large teeth away from which one is recommended to stay. However, let us not get too off-the-wall with local fauna because most every female on the planet will focus on the bête noire of the creepies: the spider. Please do not tell me there are cute spiders. That's an oxymoron if I have ever heard one, and I've heard plenty.

To start with, spiders have more legs than I can personally cope with. Combine that with a lightning turn of speed, and I am rendered catatonic. I am told that there are tarantulas that combine legs, hair, size, and a nasty bite, but personally these are some facts of which I would rather remain in semi-blissful ignorance, thank you very much. Do not show me photos of bird-eating spiders or other gruesome objects unless you wish to hasten me to an early grave, because it's really quite unnecessary. I'll get there in my own time, without your assistance. I have learned to recognize black widow spiders, but the less I have to do with even the thought of them, the better.

On my lanai there are little spiders called crab spiders—and no, they are not cute! They are just smaller versions of misery for me. I do not need to know that they are fascinating with their hard, carapace-like body. They are still spiders that scuttle everywhere faster than I can sweep them up. However, for the ordinary person living in my area, wolf spiders have got to be the most annoying. If you have the misfortune to squish one, you will regret it instantly because many of them carry packs of tiny wolf spiders within their body, which you will then have released into the world to haunt you further.

I had a resident spider way up in the corner of my cathedral ceiling for months. It was too high for me to swat, spray, vacuum, or any other forms of spider-cide that I had in mind, but it didn't matter. Charlotte, as it was dubbed, lived there happily for months, never moving as far as I knew, and never descending to wreak havoc among the humans. It was the closest I have ever come to having a household pet, albeit with many legs. The skeptics who may read this will shake their heads pityingly, thinking that the spider was long deceased and had just petrified up there in the rare atmosphere of my ceiling, but you are all so wrong. One day, Charlotte decided to go for a wee toddle and actually moved from one side of the room to the other. This new location was quite adventurous, as Charlotte was now approaching swatting range, but as I approached stealthily, swatter in hand, Charlotte scuttled back to the original oxygen-poor spot and settled back down for another couple of months before disappearing altogether.

I am a believer of out of sight, out of mind, and I can happily coexist with a many-legged critter if I cannot see it. Let them make one mistake—for instance, dropping on my face while I am still enjoying my forty winks—and mayhem is just a mild euphemism for the resulting action. It is not a pretty sight, not for the onlooker or me, and certainly not for the spider. Why do they always seem to run toward the death-dealing whirling dervish that can be observed leaping about in her nighttime jammies? Has no one explained the rule of self-preservation to them? I guess they used up all their brain cells in growing extra legs—a bad mistake, I can tell you. Let us assume that said stupid spider has now gone legs up. It still has to be swept up with many involuntary shudders, let me add. Maybe there's a spider down here in Florida that plays possum! Now that would be smart. As soon as this make-believe spider notices the approach of an instrument of death, it should roll over, forming that perfect octagonal shape of dead spider, and then endure a quick sweep into a container and removal outside, and when the heat has metaphorically died down (except here in Florida where it *never* dies down), it could unfold its legs and scuttle off to terrify others.

Luckily, I don't think such a spider is on our flora and fauna listing, for which we should all be eternally thankful.

Fashion Police!

I am of the opinion that style and fashion are at opposite ends of the scale.

As a person who has been at her most observant during the age of hot pants, maxi skirts, miniskirts, pencil skirts, and even no skirts (we wore long tops), we women really need to follow some basic rules.

One of the rules that should be learned at an early age is that if your mother looks at what you are wearing, throws her apron over her head, and disclaims all knowledge of you and what you want to wear that day, then maybe you ought to toddle off back to your room and take a long, hard look in the mirror. I and the rest of the fashion police need absolutely no training to know that a miniskirt on a body that could give a Russian shot putter a run for her money is not likely to pass muster when trying to get out of the house. For a start, models who are related to stick insects have a greater leeway when wearing skirts that I'm sure are really just oversized belts than the rest of the skirt-wearing population. When one weighs ninety pounds soaking wet, there is not a lot of spillage in the middle arena, whereas a healthier-sized person may need a little more material to drape over the excess body parts.

I am not picking on the younger set because, let's face it, they can often get away with more fashion faux pas than those of us of a more mature age. Hemlines, for instance, really need to stay below the knee as soon as one has reached the delightful age of, let's say, fifty. If you disagree, just look at the knees of your friends, grandmothers, and fellow workers who have all reached, or even surpassed fifty. Our knees just don't look like they used to. Moving on, the same goes for sleeveless tops. I don't know about you, but my upper arms have more moveable sections than a centipede. Sometimes bits move on their own without any instruction from the owner. So distressing! So please, people, whatever the popular mode of fashion is, if it involves garments that display the upper arms, try wearing it in front of a mirror, and wave your arms around. If your upper arms are still in motion a few seconds after you think you have stopped, then this garment is not for you. Trust me on this one.

I have several friends who are very proud of the fact that they are still able to wear the same outfit that they bought and wore for a function thirty years ago. Woo-hoo! Unfortunately, styles do not move with the times. Take it from me! Give the outfit away! Take a moment, cry over it, be proud of the fact that if it *was* the only garment in the world you *could* wear it, but the rest of the world really wishes you wouldn't.

I read somewhere that current fashion trends are really for the younger section of the population. Let's face it—they have the money to spend on their wardrobe because they have yet to experience mortgages, children, college loans, and other such expenses, and clever designers should gently adjust the trend so that for us more senior in the clothes-buying section, we can be modish without being members of the "mutton dressed as lamb" sorority.

I have deliberately targeted my female friends, because, let's face it, the most peculiar trend (I refuse to call it anything remotely connected with fashion) of sagging pants that display the multilayered underwear of some of today's young men should only be dealt with by their parents or a series of mirrors and does not belong on this page.

If you feel the urge to disregard the signs of a more maturing body and decide to wear what you want and tell the rest of the world to go suck a lemon, then do it with confidence. Please don't sneak around trying to pull down a hemline that was really meant as a cummerbund. Just wear the appropriate underwear and strut your stuff. Pay careful attention, readers. Wear the appropriate underwear! Granny knickers detract from the ensemble no matter how modish the garment. There will be those among us who will secretly wish that we had the front and maybe the back to wear the same design. If you can get in and out of a car without displaying what you ate for breakfast, go for it. If it sends the people immediately around you into hysterics, then it's on you. Maybe a trial run should have been the first order of the day.

Then we have the moving neckline. This should be a fashion police basic. There are those among us who are more endowed than others in the décolletage department. At a certain age, this area gets lonely and wants to join the lower parts. It manages to do this without warning, so take heed. If your endowment is more rather than less, chill out on the vivid designs. It just focuses on the direction of travel, and as the neck is immediately above this area, the less attention *that* receives, the better. Even stick-insect shapes have trouble with very low necklines. This is one time when a buxom shape carries more weight (no pun intended), but it is still not a candidate for qualifying in the louder and more colorful print contest.

One must realize that all these comments are purely a matter of personal opinion. When I think that I am dressed to kill, I choose my critics carefully. Do not ask for advice from a person whose parking space you have just pinched, nor from someone who owes you a favor. Try asking the much younger female members of the family. They have no ax to grind, unless they secretly covet what you have chosen to wear. The phrase, "Really, Mom" is a dead giveaway that it's back to the drawing board.

Basically, wear whatever you want, but be prepared for the consequences. Beware the dreaded selfie takers. You are likely to find yourself front and center in someone else's photo by accident, and the camera never lies. I have personally made more fashion blunders than I care to admit, and a large percentage have been immortalized by my starring in some form of permanent recorded photo shot. These will be produced at future gatherings and are probably recorded in the archives of the fashion police somewhere. So if you've got it, flaunt it, unless it's something sleeveless, because after you've done with it, your arms will still be moving.

Fashion police alert!

New Year Resolutions!

The New Year is upon us, and that means that the impending spate of resolutions is once again hovering in the background.

Why do we do it? Is it to make us seem as if we are made of sterner stuff than our friends and families? I am just as bad as the next person, with the slight difference being that I try to only make one resolution, so that when my resolve gets put on a shelf somewhere, I can try to kid myself that I haven't given up—I've just decided to make the whole experience last till next year. (Raucous laughter may be heard from the entire family.)

This year will be different! Instead of making a new resolution, I will take one from a few years ago and resuscitate it, thereby convincing myself that it was undergoing an annual makeover.

So which of my shelved resolutions is getting to make an appearance? Drum roll ... I am once again resolving to have as little to do with people or situations that make my day less enjoyable. Life is just too darned short. Consider the required trips to the local grocery store. We all have to do it, because the staples of life are not usually handed to us on a plate—unless you happen to be the queen, and that's a whole new discussion.

When I go to the store, several things need to happen if the whole experience is to end up on the positive side of the scale. I am assuming that I have started on the plus side by finding a parking space that's not a mile away, and I also manage to get a cart that has four wheels that will work with me. Having achieved all that, all I ask is that when I get inside the store, and I smile at someone, that someone returns the favor. We don't need to have a live debate on the state of the nation, just a smile and maybe a "good morning" if lady luck is with me. If I'm greeted with a face that would turn pickles sour, and the ensuing service offered to me is downright unhelpful with not a smile to be seen, then I will either go somewhere else or just put off what I wanted to do until another time. I am accused of being friendly to a fault, because not everyone wants to laugh like a hyena at nonsensical incidents, but I can tell you that if you are having a really rough time, try finding something to smile about. However, here's a word of caution. If the incident that shows every sign of causing you to fall about laughing involves someone else's discomfort, make sure that you've got a head start in leaving the area.

So my question is, do we have some genetic switch inside us? It's the age-old slip on a banana peel symptom that will be my downfall. I know, I know, don't laugh at someone else's misfortune, but sometimes it's just so funny. I have been known to slump helplessly in unsuppressed hysteria over the back of a chair after watching someone skid on a wet patch on the kitchen floor. If it was a dignified slip, that would be acceptable and may invoke just a slight smirk, but usually it's accompanied by wild arm flailing and some rapid foot movement that would make Riverdance seem static.

Life is full of daily happenings that can either be downright boring or just distasteful, but one doesn't have to look very far to find something or someone that will brighten one's day, and if you're lucky, it will rub off on the people you meet.

So here's my resolution for life in general. If it's going to make you feel rotten—don't do it. If you're going to regret what you said—don't say it. If you have to say it, say it with a smile. Honey wins over vinegar every time, unless you're going to make a salad dressing. Then you may need to adjust the recipe.

What's Your Name?

H ands up all those readers who think that this title is meant for a human! Well, you'd be wrong. Was it meant for maybe a four-legged member of someone's family? Nope! Guess again.

This was a question addressed to my car! I would not make this up because otherwise people in white coats are likely to read this and take me away. After watching some films where inanimate objects are given names and take on personalities, this question is becoming more and more common. There is a certain branch of my family who have incredibly bad luck with their vehicles until the respective car, truck, or motorcycle has been baptized and welcomed into the bosom of family life. Give your vehicle a name, and it becomes your special car, your method of transportation, and your traveling companion. Who else would willingly wait in the rain for you without complaining or shelter you from the hot Florida sun without passing out? Your car. Who else will protect you from midges, no-see-ums, mosquitoes, and the like? Your car. Who else will give you warnings that your driving skills need to be brushed up a little—you lane hopper, you? Your car.

Once the baptism is over, your new member of the family begins to take on his or her own personality. Sometimes this is good, and sometimes this can be embarrassingly bad. Just like humans, if you leave your car outside in the cold for too long, the car may well respond by—well—not responding. Cars need to be loved and appreciated. A little polish here and there, a tasty cocktail to clear the pipes/arteries from time to time, and occasionally for a real treat, you can feed your baby with ultra-high test fuel. The latter should only be dispensed sparingly, or else your car will react like a child with a sudden sugar rush and end up with ADHD or automatic destruction hysteria disorder. This is a well-known symptom where your precious car seems hell bent on racing everywhere, ignoring speed limits, challenging *big* trucks to see who can pull away from the traffic lights the fastest, and managing to park over a series of three marked spaces, and backwards to boot. Don't tell me that this car does not have its own personality.

My own little darling is a well-behaved small car, well trained, and I thought, tuned in to her owner's moods. My car has definite feminine traits, as you would expect from a wee red car named Ruby, and sometimes Ruby can exhibit what in a human female would be PMS, or for cars, it would be potential mechanical surrender. Well, Ruby was miffed at the world in general and me specifically. She had given me subtle hints that maybe, just maybe, the batteries that were necessary for optimum operations were starting to fail. Eventually, having lost all patience with me, Ruby waited until I was in a strange city and had parked her, locked, out in the open, but definitely where there was not a centimeter of shade anywhere. In my absence, a typical Florida storm came from nowhere, lashing all and sundry with the surprising force that is not an unusual encounter down here. I made a mad dash for Ruby, who responded by squatting there in the street in a major sulk. She refused to unlock her doors for me in spite of the torrential rain, until I was thoroughly soaked. When she considered I'd been punished enough, she graciously managed to get enough juice from somewhere to enable the doors to be opened. I have learned from experience that patience is expected when dealing with Ruby, so, resisting the urge to deliver a well-earned kick up the exhaust, I squelched into the driver's seat and waited patiently for help to arrive in the shape of another car with jumper cables. Ruby may have allowed me to unlock the door, but she was *not* going to allow me to unlock the trunk to retrieve my own cables.

Having weathered this hiccup, Ruby and I have an understanding. I don't feed her extravagant fuel, nor do I feed her rubbish. I wash her and sometimes treat her to a spa day. I change her wardrobe when her tires start to look the worse for wear. I take her for regular checkups and make sure her insurance is current. Now, gentle reader, tell me that this is an inanimate piece of metal, plastic, and rubber! There are people who don't give their kids the amount of care and attention that this car gets. Ruby is her name, and she is a member of my family, and during her life span she will be nurtured. I have tried to introduce her to other automobile members of my family, but basically, she's scared of the big trucks because they're loud and pushy, and the smaller cars are usually full of noisy humans and sometimes animals too, so Ruby is a bit of a loner.

When those little men in white coats come for me and ask me for my name, they had better be looking me square in the eyes, or else Ruby is likely to answer.

Who Is That Person?

on't you just love the term *makeover*? Admittedly, the before and after pictures of some acquaintances have been pretty spectacular, and I am left wondering about some facts of life.

By the time that one's face has been scrubbed, rinsed, massaged, toned, and peeled, what is there left? Oh yes—the removal of several layers of skin obviously isn't enough, so all the facial trimmings, such as eyebrows, eyelashes, and other unwanted hairs have to be plucked, trimmed, or permanently removed. I don't know about you, but I would be five pounds lighter by this time and certainly unrecognizable.

Then begins the laborious task of starting with a fresh palette. I understand that there are several preparatory layers that have to be applied in fairly regimented order. A moisturizer to replace all the juices that have been ruthlessly drained from your face, then concealers to conceal the fact that you may have some dark shadows somewhere, because after all, you have just got two kids off to school, fed and walked the dog, done three loads of laundry, and tried desperately to hide the fact that you have only had two hours of sleep.

Then comes the base foundation. It's bit like a layer of fine cement before you lay tiles. Now your face is totally bland and expressionless until the work begins on adding blush. (We called it rouge in my heyday, but don't judge me.)

So now the overall skin is covered with a variety of stuff, and it's time for your windows on the world to be brought out. What does that mean? I think it means that dark lines are drawn all around your eyes, and a variety of colors are judiciously added to the upper and lower lids. By now, you will be lucky if you can even open your eyes, and to add extra weight, the dreaded mascara is applied to whatever lashes you thought you had. Worry not—if you are lacking in this area, a set of false eyelashes will be glued on to your lids. One false move and your eyes will be welded shut, so pay careful attention to the person wielding the wand or to us lesser mortals, the stick with the black sticky stuff smeared on it. Your remaining eyebrows will have been plucked, waxed, and shaped to change your expression and the bald bits filled in and extended with yet another coloring stick.

I'm scared to even describe the lip area. Most of us will have earned smile lines, which is a nicer way of saying that there are crinkly vertical lines adjacent to our lips that suck in any form of coloring stick you may previously have wanted to use. Not a pretty sight, I can tell you. So now you will be introduced to lip liners. Basically, that's like a waterproof application that stops any migration of anything between your lips and the rest of the canvas. Oops! I mean face. For some reason best known to the artist, your lip liner needs to be a different color from the basic lipstick. No! I don't know why but I'm sure that I can think of a reason if I try hard enough. To finish off the lower part of this makeover, a liberal application of some gloss like glue is applied. Yes, this will cause your lips to stick together, but then you can't mess up the artwork either.

All that remains now is for your crowning glory that had been formally shampooed within an inch of its life to be cut, colored, permed, teased, or braided and coated with some form of lacquer so that if you do have to move your head, your chiseled hair will remain unmovable. Of course you will not be able to run your fingers through it either without potentially breaking one or two digits, but hey, this is a makeover! So now the final work of art is complete. Assuming you still have the strength to lift up your head so that you can see where you are going, you emerge from this day of second time around creation to present the finished work of art. If the artist has done his or her work correctly, you will be completely unrecognizable by your family and friends, who will be furrowing their brows (that have not been waxed and shaped), wondering, "Who is that person?"

Now you may wonder if perhaps a present-day Picasso has taken his palette and has been using you as a canvas. Look in the mirror! Are your eyes and other features in roughly the usual place? Yes? Then you are good to go. You have just been made over.

Please Wait to Be Seated!

I refuse to believe that the following comments are peculiar to me and mine. Having listened to the exasperated complaints that follow what should have been pleasant dining experiences for many of my acquaintances, I really think it's a national malady that is a precursor to eating out.

Picture this very familiar scenario: you and yours (or maybe just you if you can't wheedle anyone into eating with you) will select a place to have lunch, dinner, or some form of meal. Hold that thought, because it goes downhill from there on.

You thrust open the door and step inside to what seems to be a deserted restaurant. Tables and chairs are nicely set up with the requisite number of place settings, glasses, and all things associated with an eating emporium, but there is no sign of life anywhere. Your first thought is to check the opening times, because some of us have been known to get such details badly wrong. However, the lights are on, there is music playing somewhere, and you are confronted with a large sign that says, "Please wait to be seated!" Maybe hungry visitors cannot be trusted to find a table all by themselves.

After all, it's obviously an art form. When someone does eventually appear, he or she will make a big thing about carefully maneuvering his or her way through this deserted restaurant to locate a table for you. The idea that we are incapable of finding a table of which we approve all by ourselves is not taken into account, so if you are bored, you can then start the table-hopping game. (This game is not to be recommended if you are very hungry as the staff have their own games they can play too.) Don't over play your hand here as some servers are quite likely to seat you in the far corner close to the kitchen door or the entry to the rest rooms, and nearly always right underneath the AC vent that is dangling icicles from its grill.

I have been told that tables are allocated to particular servers, so the table-swapping game gets the serving staff very confused, and this may reflect in the service you get. They use sneaky little payback tricks such as forgetting to bring water until you have finished your meal and making you wait for the bill for way too long. Pick your battles.

One of my rules that I have had to share with coworkers, business associates, or even in my younger days with the current flame is this: never try to have a private conversation in a restaurant. In between the constant questions from the hovering server as to whether we are enjoying the meal, or whether we need extra bread, water, wine, or whatever, somewhere in there I lose my will to live. Remember that a restaurant is a place for eating, so give that your full attention because any attempt to conduct any other form of business is going to result in someone (usually me) getting miffed with the constant interruptions. I have never understood how secret agents manage to get a quiet table in the back corners of little restaurants, where they are left completely alone, and the business of espionage can be carried out without any interruptions at all. But then, I don't write the scripts.

In my group one of the major considerations is the ambient temperature. Living in Florida, temperatures are usually fairly high, until you set foot into a restaurant. Word to the wise—take layers of warm clothing with you because the drop in temperature when you set foot inside most restaurants will be more than significant. I don't know about you, but I don't like to hang around in places where I'm freezing my menu off, and if the ambient temperature was more conducive to enjoyment, I would be more likely to prolong my visit, have a quiet glass of whatever takes my fancy, and generally be in such a good mood that I may well tip more generously than if I'm shaking with frostbite. The standard rule that the hotter the outside, the colder will be the inside seems to prevail. I know that air conditioning is necessary, but a thirty-degree drop in temperature between the outside and the inside? Really? I have had guests relapse into a catatonic stupor because they are conserving any heat available so that they can breathe. This is where you should approach your server and politely request that they increase the inside temperature or call 911.

If the trauma of actually getting a table and a server isn't difficult enough even in a deserted restaurant, try getting out of there! Assuming you have coerced the staff to give you a bill and you have searched your conscience so that you leave an adequate tip, then plan your escape route. The inquisition you went through to even get a table in the first place is nothing to what you will encounter when trying to leave. "Was your dining experience pleasant? Would you fill out this survey? You could win five hundred dollars if you just go online and join our dining club. Would you like to join our rewards program and receive two cents back for every dollar you spend? How was your meal? Come back and see us!" Need I go on?

Yes, I know, statistics are important for some program somewhere, but I just want to pay and leave! I will try to have a great day because most people do, but it's not really under my control. However, do not try to explain this to the person who is trying to usher you out so the next group may try to get in. The next group of would-be diners are obviously lacking in training on how to distinguish between an empty table or one that is full, so they obediently stand there, blocking your escape, because we all know by now that you have to wait to be seated.

Death By Chocolate!

I do believe that if I could choose the manner of my final passing to the great candy store in the sky, it would be while being submerged in the warmth of a functioning chocolate fountain.

Seriously! I have ecstatic memories of visiting a small lunchtime café in Scotland where discerning diners were offered strawberries and cream with a hot chocolate sauce. Did this nectar come in a little warm jug? No! It came in the form of a huge chocolate fountain set up in the middle of the restaurant, and those partaking of said offering, of which I was right in the front, held their dish of strawberries under this stream of heaven for as much warm, creamy, and delicious chocolate sauce as they could fit on their dish.

I remember watching a British sitcom where the star of the program was invited to a reception that sported such a chocolatey fountain of bliss. "I'm going in!" was the battle cry, and if I had had the opportunity, I would have been right there too. In fact, I may well have employed a rugby tackle to ensure my sole rights.

I'm not totally oblivious to the dangers attached to my craving, but when I tell you, gentle readers, that if there was a college offering studies in chocolate tasting, I would have attained my master's degree long ago, if not my doctorate.

There are all sorts of titillating ways in which sales people try to help addicts such as yours truly, and for that, I am thankful, including bacon covered in chocolate and ants covered in chocolate and other forms of chocolate covered protein. If insects covered in this delectable coating are supposed to make us less likely to drool, the advertisers have got that badly wrong. You see, if we don't like what's inside, we can just melt off the chocolate, throw away the creepy center, and indulge on the good stuff.

I have often wondered why nobody has come up with a chocolate coating for pills and other nasty-tasting stuff. Even wee kiddies could be induced to take their medicine if it was hidden in a chocolate shell.

I have heard that those who have been ordained to the priesthood often bemoan the drop off in attendance of the faithful, so I wonder if the suggestion of chocolate-dipped hosts may up the numbers a little. Hmmmm. After all, red wine is a great complement to chocolate, or is it the other way round? Just a thought—for which I am likely to have to do some form of penance.

I am a very particular person. I have even been called a chocolate purist. Don't mess with my chocolate. Chocolate ice cream? I can do without. Even chocolate cake is a very poor substitute to chocolate itself. I have tried chocolate with sea salt, chocolate with spicy chili, and chocolate with nuts and fruit. All quite tasty, but you can't beat the heavenly taste of just pure chocolate. That's why a chocolate fountain is the dessert of choice in my household. Am I drooling as I type this? Yes I am. Do I have a chocolate fountain at hand? No I don't. Do I possess one? Of course I do. Should I immediately go and turn my fountain on? Yes I should. I have to have something to sustain myself between breakfast and elevenses so as soon as the machine tells me the fountain of life (or death) is ready, "I'm going in."

About the Author

Valerie Crowe has several published children's books to her credit, and has lately added a humorous collection of personal experiences to her repertoire.

Since relocating to the United States, she enjoys a busy retirement writing in Palm Harbor. She is the author of The Precious Knights series as well as 'Who Put Ice In My Tea?'

Printed in the United States
By Bookmasters